THE INFINITE BEAUTY OF REALITY

THE INFINITE BEAUTY
OF REALITY

Selected Poems by
Vijay Pal Singh

Accents Publishing • Lexington, Kentucky • 2025

Printed in the United States of America

Accents Publishing
Editor: Katerina Stoykova
Individual poems edited by Mary Margaret Adams
Cover Image: Carolyn Singh, *Reflections*, 2025

Library of Congress Control Number: 2025949123
ISBN: 978-1-961127-20-3
First Edition

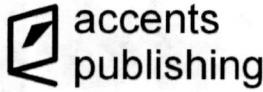

accents
publishing

Accents Publishing is an independent press for brilliant voices. For a catalog of current and upcoming titles, please visit us on the Web at

www.accents-publishing.com

CONTENTS

Were Vijay here, he would dedicate this book to:

His family and friends.

He would have wonderful things to say about each one of them.

*And to all those who with a steadfast heart and soul fire
dare to act out their most noble and cherished dreams.*

But let his poems speak—

IN MY MEDITATIONS

In my meditations, I fly high
As Shiva himself, in the endless sky
I am free of the bounds of space
And free of the bounds of time
I am bathed in light that I myself emanate
It is cool to the touch yet immeasurably bright

BY THE SEA

In my mind within and in the mind without,
The light of sunrise; orange first and then white,
In the sky, the vast horizon in the distance;
In the near collision of the land and the ocean,
In the eyes and ears, heavy with sleep, there is
The ancient sound of waves breaking on the ground
All seems as it should be; in harmony
With the whole of the universe
Varied noises; a song on the radio, a child's laughter, a cry of a dove,
All merge in this peaceful repose of mind,
This river of grace from heaven above
In the fountain of joy, sprouting from the spring of unconditional love

THE REAL I

Sometimes, in an exhale,
I become myself,
My mind, set free, expands
Into the infinities outside

Universes sail along,
Like an ocean over the shore,
Light spreads across the horizon;
And in the air, a melody flows

KALEIDOSCOPE

The earth is not turning
The sun is not rising
It's just apparitions
In consciousness
Rearranging themselves

ALL IN THE MIND

I once told you, Vijay Pal
In this moment
The choice is yours
You can make it bliss filled
Or another occasion for torment

KINDNESSES FORGOTTEN / CRUELTIES REMEMBERED

Sadly, cruelties are remembered
And relived over and over
But acts of love and kindness,
Generally more ubiquitous,
Are thought to be intrinsically deserved
Hence of little consequence,
Obviously not worthy of gratefulness
Or worse, not even noticed at all
Due to a lack of mindfulness

DREAMY SIDE

Cherish it, nourish and protect it,
From realists, self-styled,
This gift, most precious,
The dreamy side of life

After years wasted
On groundless fears, misguided pursuits,
And unnecessary guilt,
It now appears to me
That the dreamy part,
Is most, if not all, of me

The rest, just sleepwalking

GOAL OF LIFE

In a cool summer breeze,
With light on aspen leaves
Sings the essence of existence

Superposed on that
Is the theater;
Built by thought and language,
It puts food on the table
And keeps tedium at bay

The show must go on,
Say the elders
For someday, the goal
Might come into sight

Meanwhile, if the journey be enthralling,
Then the destination
May as well be imaginary

WAVES OF THOUGHT

Deep from the womb of the ocean
You and I, we watch the sun rise
This summer morning on the cool shore
Reflections off the water play hide and seek
All drowns in the mesmerizing rhythm
As mighty waves rise high with the tide
In this tattva of Shiva pure and sweet

You and I, the waves of thought we ride
To kingdoms very far away we go
Where colors dance and music flows
Time goes both ways, as does space
Now we are of light, and now we have a face

ENLIGHTENMENT OF MAN

Enlightenment for a wave is for her to realize
That she is the same as the mother ocean
If that seems too abstract or too far-fetched
Then she might want to know that she is the same
As the water she ebbs and heaves, the water,
Which is seemingly endless; here, there, and everywhere

Enlightenment of man is for him to realize
That he is the same as the mother cosmos
If that seems too abstract and too far-fetched
Then he might want to know that he is the same
As the air he inhales and exhales, the air,
Which is seemingly endless; here, there, and everywhere

DANCE

Is it the wind
That dances the eagle?
Or is it the eagle
That dances the wind?

Round and round they go
In circles large and small
In the precious ecstasy of just being
For a long while, time comes to a stall

TIMES ORDINARY

Times ordinary that fill the daily round
Are very precious, in fact, quite profound
Heavenly confluences of human love and God's grace
Their value comes into focus, when illness stares us in the face

OUR TIME

The age of this universe
Is neither six thousand years
Nor thirteen point eight billion,
But just this instant of the light on a dewdrop,
As the earth turns and the sun appears on the horizon

Billions of years are rolled
Into this moment now present

How sweet then
That you loved me
For so many dewdrops

WANDERINGS

Many think me deficient
For not wanting this or that
Ignorant of what, why, and how
But for me, it's enough
To wander free and undirected
In this life of eternal now

THE JEWEL

Never was there a need to fight the cosmic current
So embrace the time, this jewel, the present moment
Look at the light now, so luminous, ubiquitous
Let it free you, fly you into space infinite, continuous

SWEET IS THE MORNING

In the window, it's morning
Day has come to wake the night
From its long, lazy, languor
Dream of a forgotten longing

In a compact, as old as earth
Light has come from far in space
Arriving now to embrace the waiting ground
Igniting the forest with new sight, sweet sound

I celebrate the nature that gives life its fullness
Glory be to the sun that obliterates the darkness
Newspapers speak of war, pestilence, greed, and sorrow
Fresh worries of what new worries might come tomorrow

But here, there is just me, the ground, and the light
And God, gentle, in his infinite might

TRANSIENT INTENSITY

Replete is literature, and culture,
With a longing for love so profound
That it would transcend time, thus lifting the screen,
Revealing reality in its full resplendent beauty

Why then is such love not more common?
Could it be that it is indeed present everywhere?
Yet we fail to perceive it, because we have a wrong sign;
Steady permanence, instead of its preferred state of intense transience?

Love is revealed directly in intensity,
But, in duration, only by extrapolation

The Canyon in Arizona, dug by the Colorado
May well be grand, ancient, and rare
But it is the lightning that reveals divinity,
In a burst of energy with direct immediacy

Shiva, who abhors boredom,
Made change fundamental to his creation;
It behooves us, therefore to not only accept change as inevitable,
But also to embrace it as we would a lover,
Celebrate it as ancients did the changing of seasons
And further, educate our children to worship
Not only the word for its seeming permanence,
But also, the river for her flowing presence

LABOR OF LOVE

The sun does not burn
To earn a living

He just lives
In the lightness of being

THE MELTING

Galloping, horse and rider are each other
As they together melt into the rhythm

Gliding, fish and river are each other
As they together melt into the water

Soaring, eagle and sky are each other
As they together melt into the air

In love, you and I are each other
As we together melt into Spandalahar

MORE TO THE POINT

It seems now that we are parted
We are two bodies separate in space and time
But from the way you are in my dreams
And the songs of love that you sing in my mind
I know that we are one; playing two just for fun
Some days the act goes too far; we even forget to return
Such is our love; real now, and now just a play, a fantasy
More to the point, it helps me live in a state of deep ecstasy

COMPROMISE

Well, in some other lifetime, then,
When you and I would be braver

This time around you win;
Within the laws of men and women, we will live

This is a pretty good life, they say,
House, cars, children, and trips abroad

And after all, traces of godliness can be found
Even in the most common ordinariness around

WHEEL OF FORTUNE

A Time Lord once,
I am now
Just a plain man

Still, sometimes
The magic returns

Best to accept less, they say
But over the horizon,
I keep looking out for you

JEWELS OF LOVE

Such precious loves
I have had
Each one a jewel
To cherish and treasure

And if the intensity
Was less than infinite,
The texture of time
Less than exquisite,

It was only my fault
For suffering baseless fears,
And overarching greed;

The cruel stupidity
Of trading the present
For future cravings

Far too often mistaken
For the romantic notion
Of reaching for dreams

In fact, the latter
Is different altogether;
Such as the difference between
A long-view stock investor
And a desperate day trader

HAPPY LIVES

I.

Marked by love intense, moderate worldly success,
Good karma and good dharma,
Many fine lives have I lived in this lifetime
Some were only a moment in duration,
Others, two or three, or more
Many were filled with ecstasy, others with joy,
Yet others with ordinary happiness
A few were forgettable and a few others just a bore

II.

Do most men have happy lives or was I especially lucky;
An exception with more than the average share?
If so, it must have been good luck or sincerity,
Good karma or, most likely, just plain grace,
For I was not the cleverest of chess champions,
Nor the runner with the fastest pace

III.

Now the light on the dew on the leaves,
Light in the trees, light in the grass, and light in my mind,
All bid me to come home and be of light yet again
So dear family, friends, lovers, and others
I thank you with all of my heart
And bid goodbye, for it's time to depart
True, there are a few promises still outstanding,
But sorry, I must now take a pass

INTENSE TRANSIENCE

Love, as with other concepts of importance,
Is imbued by elders with the virtue of permanence

One might think that a thing so fundamental
Would be ubiquitous, but it is not so
In fact, love lasting forever is so rare that
One wonders if it is even humanly possible

Could it be that the elders made an error;
That love is plainly visible everywhere,
Failure to see it caused not by its rarity
But the difficulty with virtue ill assigned?

At the core of its essence is not permanence,
But very intense transience;
As in lightning versus redwood trees,
Or the Colorado carving the Grand Canyon

Lightning, packing energy and divinity
Not lesser than the redwood tree, is not rare
Similarly, love, intense and unconditional,
At first sight or at another instant, later
Is so common that it is foolishly forgotten,
Not sufficiently celebrated in art and song,
Often, even, degraded at the altar of permanence

I TO MYSELF

Thus, the other day said I to myself:

Born from unfettered awareness
A single instant of perfect clarity
Sliding effortlessly into the next instant
Would fling open the window of time
Onto the infinite beauty of reality
Your heart will overflow with gratefulness
Your knees will bend and hands come together
In a spontaneous posture of religious piety

Having just one such moment would be a victory
Rendering your whole life meaningful
And better still, as if icing on a cake that's already fine
Would be the sharing of one such moment
With the one you love, among humans, a goddess divine

So, the other day said I to myself

JOYFUL EXISTENCE

Living is more than the suspension of disbelief
In the seeming purposelessness of this universe;
It is spontaneous, absorptive, and immersive participation
Moment by moment and breath by breath
In the joy that is existence

There are times when this joy becomes self-evident
As when one is transported by music
Or when one lets go and goes with the flow
Of the river or the flow of existence
Actually, the joy is present all the time;
It's just that often times it gets camouflaged
By an excessive desire for the joy in the future
Or by an excessive regret for the joy missed out in the past

NOT SAD

In billowy waves
Castles in the sand are erased
This is not sad
For in the intervals
New dreams are made

THIS LIFE

Now Shiva exhales; from darkness, worlds emerge
Energy and intelligence create, consume, and regenerate;

Green of grass; blue of sky; breeze from the sea;
Wind on the prairie; mountain's stubbornness; flow of the river;
Projects of insects; fight and fright in reptiles;
Nurture among mammals; birds reaching for the sky;
Song, music, dance, poetry, and meditation

Some billions of years later, Shiva inhales
All is darkness, worlds submerge; everything descends;

The selfless giving of mothers; sacrifices of fathers; generosity
    of teachers;
Songs of poets; genius of scientists; self-importance of traders;
Conceit of preachers; and the cruelty of the self-righteous

NEW MEXICO GHOSTS

Diggers are gone
And the silver and gold
Of these ghost towns
Lost
The mountain reigns
And the streets
Have no names

WITNESS OR OBSERVER

Thunderstorms come
Then are suddenly gone
Rivers are born
Then one day run dry
All the while
The light in the sky
Just continues to smile

IRISES

In the septic bed
Irises bloom
An abundance
Of purple glory

Shit happens
And beauty thrives

RUBBISH OUTSIDE

This morning,
Wandering
In the sparkles
Of Spandalahar
I ran into my Self
Of another time,
Another life

You are better,
Much better
Than I thought,
Said I to my Self
Why, you seem divine!
So were you, always,
He replied,
But you forgot to pay attention to your Self
And listened instead to the dribble outside

FLASH OF ENCHANTMENT

In the bazaar of distant antiquity
Crowded, swarming, noisy, and dirty
Men and women talk in endless chatter
Forever parsing this or that important matter

In the midst of a thousand chores
Suddenly, a sweet quiet at the core
A sense of wellness in daylight's beam
Primal and pure as a mountain stream

LAND OF THE FREE

What if you lived
In the land of the free
And the home of the brave
But did not know it
Much less feel it
Or be it?

Maybe you could
Find someone to blame
Father, mother, teachers,
Preachers, or top one percenters

Or could you
Do something
to fix the situation
And be brave
And free?

What if you found out
That the land of the free
And the home of the brave
Was in fact your Mind?

Would you then
Wait for help
From father, mother, teachers,
Preachers, or top one percenters?

Or would you
Do something
To fix the situation
And be brave
And free?

OLD DELHI

I once saw
In old Delhi
A young boy
The same age as I was
Waiting for me
To finish eating a banana
So he could eat
What was left
In the throwaway peel
Maybe now you can see
Why I am not impressed
By your rather minor
Anxieties and griefs

REMEMBERING

I.

Forest grove
Out the window,
Branches sway;
Light and shade
Dance on grass

In this moment
That is what I am

II.

Organ Mountain
Breeze in face,
Cacti bloom;
Desert below
Miles on miles
Of white sand

In this moment
That is what I am

III.

Crest trail,
Sierra Blanca;
In the wind
Aspens sing,
Forest sighs

In this moment
That is what I am

IV.

Treasure Island,
Sunset on the Gulf

On the computer
Chopin Romance

In this moment
That is what I am

V.

Stinging cold of January,
New Delhi
On a cot, Yash and Pitajee
Soak the warmth;
Blinding sunshine;
The courtyard of my youth

In this moment
That is what I am

FAMILY

Childhood Sunday
Pusa, New Delhi
In torrents, it rains
Summer heat evaporates

We sit on the veranda
Relishing and marveling at
Intermittent lightning,
And the rolling thunder

On the cots, my father,
We brothers and sisters,
Ammajee* in the kitchen,
Frying pakoras

Pitajee** is pleased,
Minutes go by
Nobody speaks

Sitting together
Is sufficient

We are enveloped
In this bliss
Of silent peace

And the sacred belief
That we love each other

---

*   Ammajee: In Hindi, "Mother"
**   Pitajee: In Hindi, "Father"

CHILDHOOD IN DELHI HEAT

A hot June afternoon
Not a leaf moves
Adults cool off in a siesta
But the boy wants to play
So he ventures out into the heat
He waits, and waits some more
For a mate to come outside
To play marbles, hockey, or to climb a tree
Any game would do
Seemingly hours pass, but no one shows
All have the common sense to avoid the heat
Or parents who are in the way
But the boy is patient even though
Just five Jamun trees of Pusa
Are his only companions
Among them, he can daydream
For a very, very long time!

IT CAN HAPPEN AGAIN

Seems like when I was a child
I could daydream the whole day
There was no sense of waste, guilt, or pain
There was elation in a cone of ice cream
And in finding a friend to play with, or even simpler
In just running free in the pouring rain

Now, in the midst of a world turned busily complex, selfish,
      and almost cynical
I keep going, thinking that if it happened once, surely
      it can happen again

DESPERATION

There was always wealth enough and time enough,
And never a sense of desperation,
When I was a child, living carefree in my father's house
But now desperate men are everywhere
So much so, that desperation seems to be in the air
However, I don't need to be desperate
I can choose, to myself, to be kind,
Be the master of my own house;
Reclaim all remaining moments of my life,
Shed self-imposed responsibilities,
And also the soul-smothering daily grind

I can learn from the cat asleep on the couch,
Perfectly at home in my house,
Actually, just as much in his mind, his house;
He sleeps deeply when he sleeps,
Acts swiftly when he acts;
Always focused on his purpose, he is never desperate
Neither kind, nor unkind, he is in tune with nature,
And seems just fine being feline

ARRIVING

Even as a child I knew that one day
An ascetic monk or enlightened yogi, I would be

Seer of Reality, I would want for nothing,
Be able to move freely,
Assume different forms and bodies;

Close my eyes and, with exhales,
Like Shiva, create universes;
And with each inhale, draw them in

And lo that time has arrived!
This very moment, here on the palisades
Of the Kentucky River

All needs fulfilled; my mind is calm
Body strong; breathing uniform, easy
Childhood relived fills the heart with grace,
And from a fountain within, bliss spouts

Could it be that the monk part was not necessary?

SONS AND DAUGHTERS

The reason we have sons and daughters
Is that they make it straightforward, easy as pie
The million acts of love unconditional
Each with its own natural high

PRIMAL MOTHER

In a trajectory that seems eternal
Round and around goes the earth
Around the sun, our primal mother

Now she tilts, lilts, and spins on an axis of her own
Moving as if spiraling in a long, blissful dance
Who can tell if this be just mindless motion
Or a meaningful, mindful, and mysterious trance?

Is our world just dumb matter or a fine design of intelligence?
Or does the question betray self-created and collective ignorance?
The answer, as an elephant in the room, is so perfectly obvious
To all those who are at ease in the cosmos, and in peace
    with the universe

FIELDS AND WAVES

Waves; electric, magnetic, and electromagnetic
Are not stopped by medium or lack of it
Through air, water, walls, skin, flesh, and bones they traverse
Coursing the skin of metal, they get around

Why then do some think that the Waves of Consciousness,
Which are the essence of our body, mind, and soul,
All of ourselves and the cosmos,
Are blocked or bounded by our skin?

HOW ELSE

How else could it be except that I, like the universe,
Am of the waves of light and intelligence?
There are, sadly, long stretches of forgetfulness,
But reminders come along, gentle yet insistent,
Wafting now on the sound of the wind in the trees,
And riding, later, the crests of waves on the sea,
Pulsating at other times in the stillness of long summer afternoons
Or ringing in the ears, thoughts, and verses,
Which later grow into poetry

RAINBOW IN THE MIRROR

I know now how in the mirror there is a rainbow of colors;
It is so because my face is lit inside and out, with a light so intense,
    so bright
That she broke into her real colors and forgot that she was once white

REALITY

It is smaller than can be thought,
Also, larger than we can conceive

In at least two directions, likely more,
Our reality extends all the way to infinity

Little wonder then that it should be
So hard to wrap our heads around it

COME THEN

Come then, let us resume the ancient quest
Our long journey to the state of nirvana
For the sun is bright and the hour is right
You can bring the body or just the inner light

Of course, you can linger if you be not yet weary
Of this world that, to me, is no longer cheery
While other worlds call, enchanting, half real and half imaginary
I am ready but can still wait some more; just do not unnecessarily tarry

GOOD LIFE

Don't interrupt the music, let it flow
In love and kindness, let us all glow
Just for a moment, let us be brave
Drop all cares, ride the tallest wave

GOOD HEALTH

Good health
Is like a razor's edge:
Heaven on one side,
On the other side, hell!

ASK NOT

Ask not for whom the sun shines
As it shines for you

Ask not for whom the river flows
As it flows for you

Ask not for whom the time was made
As it was made for you

Earth may no longer be the center of the universe
But you still are

IN THE FLOW

Things happen
As they like
Not always as I want
So, I do
What needs to be done

MOVING ON

Sometimes I think of
Going to see old friends;
Then I realize that
Time has flowed;
They would rather be
Doing something else

There is a price
To the moving on

BEST I CAN

I am not much, they say;
And it's true that
My faculties are finite
However, if there is ever
A time when for you
I can do some good
Know this: I would

MARK IT

This is the time
This is the place
And in the mirror
My form and face

In this moment
Of sunshine
All is well
And I am in a state
Of contentment

I will mark this moment
Remember it well
And know that there is nothing
That I want,
Except for what is here, now

And so it is that I am ready;
Open to all adventures, and
Also, for the end of adventures

ASHES

When my body has died
Please burn it and scatter the ashes
To the wind and river

For in addition to dust to dust,
It would be nice to be
Water to water
Light to light;
Air to air

VALUE

Near the end of your life
How much would you pay
For this moment of forest shine?

FAREWELL

All things end
So, one day
Leave you I must
But then let us depart
As infinite light
Instead of
Just dust to dust

JAPANESE HAIKU

Thunderstorms have stopped
Last clouds are gone
We sit, the old mountain and I
Until only the mountain remains

THIS WORLD AND I

At each inhale,
I am of flesh;
At each exhale,
I am of light

So it is that I
Live forever
One breath
At a time

ACKNOWLEDGMENTS

I find it very difficult to speak for my much beloved husband, Vijay Pal Singh (1947-2022). I am not a writer. So, please bear with me.

When Vijay died very suddenly that September of 2022, he was working on his sixth collection of poetry, "Idle Musings" as he called all his poems. This is not that book.

He had not yet selected or ordered anything. No outlines or hints, guides—nothing at all was found among his papers to indicate what he was planning. It fell to his long-time editor/media assistant, Mary Margaret Adams, to take the boxes of loose paper, thumb drives, notebooks, odd scraps of paper, occasional napkins, and file folders of poems to transcribe and sort through. I will be forever thankful to her for her dedication, doggedness, and expertise. And her emotional support. She took on a burden I simply could not carry.

Our young friend, Amelia Long, it turns out is a writer and agent. She very graciously agreed to find places to publish Vijay's poems. She also looked for a book publisher. I am grateful for her diligence and foresight.

This led to Katerina Stoykova and Accents Publishing. Vijay attended Poesia: Lexington Workshop for several years. He loved that group and the poets who attended. The group was started by Katerina, and it has flourished. He admired and respected Katerina. She agreed to take on the project. Of the several hundred poems she was sent, she has chosen eighty to include in this volume. I cannot adequately express my gratitude to her for all she has done.

My studio assistant (I am a visual artist), Yolitzy Gorostieta, got the cover image translated into proper jpg format for printing. Thankfully I can always count on her to do the job right.

This is that book.

Carolyn Singh.
Lexington Kentucky, 2025

ABOUT THE AUTHOR

Vijay Singh was a research scientist by professional training. All of his degrees were in electrical engineering: a Ph.D. and M.S. from the University of Minnesota, Minneapolis, and a B. Tech. from the Indian Institute of Technology (I.I.T.), Delhi, India. He has made pioneering research contributions in solar cell devices, nanotechnology, electronic displays and sensors. This work is published in more than 100 articles in scientific journals and has resulted in several patents. Before retiring, Vijay was the Robinson Chair Professor in the Department of Electrical and Computer Engineering, and the Director of the Center for Nanoscale Science and Engineering at the University of Kentucky.

Although an accomplished and accredited research scientist and professor in his professional life, Vijay was a true poet at heart. He wrote thousands of poems on finding the meaning and beauty in the present moments, while simultaneously taking comfort in the eternity of being. His writings were profoundly influenced by his strong connections to family, friends, nature, and his belief in eternity. While his research and professional work was very important to him, his poetry and his relationships with others were equally as important. Ever the optimist, Vijay's poetry is meant to uplift and inspire his readers.

Vijay met his wife, Carolyn Diana Schmitz Singh at the University of Minnesota when they were both students there. Carolyn is a professional artist with a B.A. and B.F.A. degree from the University of Minnesota. They have two sons and four grandchildren.

www.ingramcontent.com/pod-product-compliance
Lightning Source LLC
Chambersburg PA
CBHW050904120626
46554CB00003B/998